Meditation and Prayers on 101 Names of God

By
Michael Kovitz

PublishAmerica

Baltimore

© 2005 by Michael Kovitz.
All rights reserved. No part of this book may be reproduced, stored in a retrieval system or transmitted in any form or by any means without the prior written permission of the publishers, except by a reviewer who may quote brief passages in a review to be printed in a newspaper, magazine or journal.

First printing

ISBN: 1-4137-4794-9
PUBLISHED BY PUBLISHAMERICA, LLLP
www.publishamerica.com
Baltimore

Printed in the United States of America

Foreword

The 101 names of God that are the subject of this book derive from a misty antiquity, but they retain a remarkable freshness even today. They form part of the ancient Zoroastrian prayer compilation known as the *Khordeh Avesta*, which can be traced back at least 2000 years, and is traditionally associated with the Prophet Zoroaster himself.[1] These names are all in Old Persian, an Indo-European language with close affinities to Sanskrit. These names also continue to form part of the regular Zoroastrian litany of prayers, both among Zoroastrians in Iran and Parsis of India.[2]

The great modern spiritual teacher, Meher Baba (1894-1969), periodically drew attention to these 101 names of God as an important spiritual legacy from the Zoroastrian tradition, and he occasionally would have them recited alongside prayers from Christian, Hindu, Muslim, and Sikh sources. Meher Baba would certainly have recited these divine names during his youth, as he grew up in the Parsi community of Pune in Western India. But in an important declaration about this prayer given in 1963, Meher Baba also emphasized that these 101 names can be an effective prayer of divine love, regardless of one's religious affiliation. Meher Baba gives both in the original Old Persian and in the translation the list of 101 names contained in this book.

These 101 Persian names of God invite comparison with the well-known 99 names of God from the Islamic tradition. All of those are in Arabic, and are taken from the descriptions of God found in the Qur'an. Recitation of these names, and meditation on their divine qualities, forms a central part of the Sufi mystical practice of *dhikr* or recollection of God.[3] Recitation of those names is considered to imbue the reciter with the divine qualities contained within the names.

A glance of the table of contents of this book will indicate some of the distinctive characteristics of the 101 names of God from Zoroastrian tradition. Some names emphasize God's transcendence beyond human comprehension: Without Beginning, Without End, Exalted One, Detached from All, Formless, Lord Invisible. Other names speak of God's infinite power and knowledge in relation to the world: Lord of All, In Touch with All, Bountiful One, Lord of the Universe. Still other names reflect on the intimate relationship between God and creation: Worthy of Our Profound Thanks, Remover of Affliction, Bountiful Giver, and Preserver of Creation. There is a particular emphasis on the profoundly ethical teachings of Zoroaster, summarized in the triple formula of "good thoughts, good words, and good deeds." This stress on truth and justice is revealed in divine names such as Never Deceiving, Just Accountant, and Lord of Just Rewards. These names of justice are matched by other names stressing divine mercy, including Forgiver of Sins, Infinitely Patient, and Compassionate Judge. An especially interesting series of names (beginning at No. 61) describes the cosmic role of God as the Transmuter of one element into another. In the end, God remains unique in his beauty: Rayed in Glory, Haloed in Light. It is significant that the very first of the 101 names is Worthy of Worship.[4]

Michael Kovitz brings to bear his own creative interpretation in the meditations on the 101 divine names that comprise this book. He draws upon spiritual symbolism from a variety of sources, including Hindu, Christian, Sufi, and Buddhist themes. An accomplished musician and poet, he reflects with sincerity and passion upon the divine qualities inherent in these names. I hope that this book of meditations will bring this remarkable ancient prayer to a new and appreciative audience.

Carl Ernst,
Zachary Smith Professor
Department of Religious Studies
University of North Carolina-Chapel Hill

Introduction

It was my intention from the beginning, that with regard to content, I would engage the process with as few preconceptions of what the work would, could, or should be. Mostly, I did not even think about a Name before I sat down to write and, on occasion, even surprised myself by what was inspired in the moment of writing. Sometimes, however, I would glance at a Name before taking our Greyhound Nazar for his morning walk, and then write about it when we returned home. None of the meditations and prayers have been fundamentally altered or changed since the original writing.

With regard to the question of style and form, I was equally as laissez-fare. Though I was not attempting to write poetry, I felt that the work was, at times, poetic in its shape, and so I allowed myself to spontaneously either use or ignore poetic convention wherever it seemed appropriate.

Capitalization is always an issue when the writing abounds with divine names, themes, and attributes. Some decisions are more obvious than others and can be determined by convention, while others seem to necessitate some kind of judgment call.

In the case of *Meditation and Prayers on 101 Names of God,* the situation was further complicated by the fact that the same, name, theme, or attribute in different meditations or prayers, seemed to call for different treatment. I have tried my best to respond to this question within the unique framework of each individual meditation or prayer and hope that my readers are not too troubled by some of the inconsistencies of my decisions.

Finally, since my use of italics often goes beyond conventional application, it may be helpful to mention that it is always employed to suggest a voice other than the voice that is, at the moment, speaking. This voice could be a quotation from another source, or another voice of the author other than the voice that is speaking at that time.

Michael Kovitz

From the Author

In reading *Meditation and Prayers on 101 Names of God*, one finds references and imagery drawn from Vedantic, Sufi, Christian, Buddhist, and Mystic sources—a reflection of my personal path and my search. Also, there are references and quotes attributed to Meher Baba, who translated the original *101 Names of God* from the ancient Persian of Zoroaster into the English language.

Meher Baba is my spiritual guide and master. He is the inspiration behind all of my writings and He is the Beloved whom I address in each of the Names.

Yet, it is my intention and also my prayer, that *Meditation and Prayers on 101 Names of God* be for all seekers of truth and lovers of God, no matter what their spiritual path or their persuasion, and it is my most sincere hope that in the reading of the Names, all may find inspiration and a renewed vigor upon their own unique and personal journey to awakening.

Michael Kovitz

"If you repeat this prayer with Love, no other prayer remains to be said…. Anyone can repeat these names with Love, irrespective of the religion he belongs to."

—Meher Baba, Poona, India, 2-4-63

Contents

Yazad... Worthy of Worship

Only You are worthy of worship
for all else is illusion and how can we worship illusion?
Respect, admiration, and appreciation, are tributes paid to creation
for maintaining the path to Your Door.
Oh Yazad, help me to traverse the path
that I might know You as You are.

Harvesp-tawan... All Powerful

Power is the capacity for action.
Action is instigated by thought.
Thought is instigated by desire.
Desire originates in Whim.

God's Whim is to know Himself and with this Knowing comes Bliss.
Since this Knowing is Infinite, this Bliss is also Infinite.
With this Knowing comes Power.
Since this Knowing is Infinite, this Power is also Infinite.

When God knows Himself
He finds Himself to be,

All Knowledge
All Power
All Bliss.

Harvesp-Agah... All- Knowing

Light passing through darkness becomes color,
color passing through experience becomes ignorance,
ignorance passing through experience becomes consciousness,
consciousness passing through experience becomes light.

Beyond light and darkness,
color and ignorance,
consciousness and experience,
is the Source of all.
The One
The All Knowing.

Harvesp-Khoda... Lord of All

All means all, big and small,
Everything and Nothing too.

You and I, and everyone—
plants and worms, fish and birds,
animals too,

Lord of all
angels and archangels, gurus and saints,

Lord of creation,
the three worlds too.

Lord of all.

Abadeh... Without Beginning

Never born,
Uncreated,
Eternal Existence.

You always were,
You always are,
and You always will be.

You were before the beginning,
and even before the beginningless beginning.

All of time is a speck of dust
lost in Your depths.

Contemplating Your Beginninglessness,
I am at peace.

Abi-Anjab... Without End

Never were You not,
ever will You be,
contemplating Your endlessness,
I am at peace.

In the beginning was the Word,
and what began in the beginning,
will end in the end.

But the One who spoke the Word,
in the end remains,

Always,
Endless,
Eternal.

Bun-e-stiha... Root of Creation

Beginningless and Endless One,
You command the beginning and the end,
and all existence in between.

You forge the link between
the infinite and the finite,
and through that link
bring life to Your creation.

You are the Hub,
circled by numberless stars.

You are the Pole of creation,
Who alone bears the weight of it all.

Frakhtan-taih… Endless Bliss

I have known the thrill of success, the fire of passion,
and a peaceful mind free of worry.
I have known happiness—but what of Bliss?

Once, You allowed me to gaze into a pure heart's soul,
and in that timeless moment,
I beheld the mystery of pain and joy
mingled in a drop of the sea
of Fraktan-taih… Endless Bliss.

Jamaga... Primal Cause

Absolutely still,
before cause and time.

Absolutely still,
before form and effect.

Then, stirred by your Whim,
Stillness sang the First Song.

Everything heard and replied,
"I am God."

But Nothing could not hear,
and began composing
endless verses to itself.

Prajtarah... Exalted One

Exalted One,
Highest of the High,
what possibility exists to lift You higher?

Yet, in my mind I build alters,
and teetering on tiptoes and stretching my arms,
I try to place You higher and higher.

Still, You seem to encourage me,
and so I have begun to wonder,
"Who is raising who?"

Oh Exalted One,
without need of exaltation,
in Your Mercy I am exalted in your Exaltation.

Tum-afik... Purest of the Pure

Free of lust, anger, greed,
hatred, jealousy, selfishness and pride,
You are the Purest of the Pure.

Oh, Unsullied One,
give me a glass of the Wine of Your Purity,
that I might raise it to my lips
to learn its taste,
and acquire the desire of it
above all lesser wines.

Abarvand... Detached from all

My detachment is separation,
but in this separation is attachment.

Your Detachment is a gesture of Your Love
That binds You to everyone and everything.

Oh Abarvand,
what kind of Detachment is this
that forever binds You to us in Your Compassion
and forever binds us to You in Your Mercy?

Parvandeh... In Touch with All

All Knowing, Infinitely Knowing,
the Knower of the past, the present, and the future.

Because Your Knowing is perpetual
You are always In Touch with All.

Oh Parvandeh,
help me walk across the bridge of Your Knowing
to become perpetually established
in remembrance of You.

An-ayafeh… Unattainable

My efforts fall short,
You are unattainable by deed or word or thought.

Austerities and devotions cannot attain You,
neither love nor violence can beat down Your Door.

Oh An-ayafeh,
You have given us the secret saying,
I am attained when you cease to exist—
when you and I are not we—but One.

Unattainable One,
lift the veil of You and me
so that I may attain the Unattainable.

Hama-Ayafeh... Attainer of All

Before the beginning,
Your Deep Sleep was disturbed
by the Whim to attain Yourself.

So, You embarked upon the Journey to Awakeningand You began to
dream
and in that dream You created me,
and took me to be Yourself.

Now, as me, You wish to awaken.

Oh Unattainable One and Attainer of All,
You alone exist
and only You can attain Yourself.

Adro… Most Righteous

Greatest of warriors,
when You unleash the arrows from Your Bow,
the mark is never missed.

When in battle,
You unsheathe Your Terrible Sword,
the enemy never escapes demise.

Greatest of warriors,
always respecting Divine Law,
when You take aim at the Final Target of Yourself
and let Your arrows fly,
the contest is never lost,
and in death You win
the deathlessness of the Righteous.

Gira... Upholder of All

You uphold the righteous and the good,
sustain love through Love,
and bear the suffering of those who long for You.

Sinners too, are upheld by You,
and the forces of lust, anger, greed,
hatred, jealousy, selfishness, and pride also.

Oh Gira,
You are the Pole that bears the canopy of all creation.
You are the Upholder of All

A-chem… Beyond Reason

Reason can never know Reality,
because reason is in the child of illusion,
and Reality is beyond illusion.

Reason is limited by mind,
and You are beyond mind.

Once upon a time,
You dropped a hint of Your Existence
and made me curious.
In time, my curiosity transformed into longing,
And oneness with You became my obsession.
I called you my Beloved,
but what can I do?

My mind continues to build highways and byways
I am convinced will lead to Your Door,
But the paths circle back and I am left again
in the place I first began.

Now, my cause has become my plight,
And I wonder,
will I ever win this fight?

Oh Achem,
Lift me to that holy consciousness
where in Reality You abide,
to that Bliss beyond all reason
to the heart beyond the mind.

Chamana... Sovereign Reason

You are the Dreamer who dreams the dream,
the Lord of mind and heart.

Over stars and planets You Reign Supreme,
in Your Heavenly Darbar.

The greatest and smallest,
most near and far,
You Rule within and above.

Oh Chamana, Sovereign Reason,
You are Emperor Supreme in the Court of Love.

Safana... Bountiful One

The gift of Your Majesty
leaves me breathless
and in the Glory of Your Power
I am effaced.

The gift of Your Compassion and Your Mercy
evoke tears of love that fill an ocean
I long to drink until I drown.

And in the vastness of Your Silence,
my mind is lost and cannot think,
and from my heart there flows a language,
that in unspoken words proclaim,

Glory, Glory, Oh Safana,
so generous and sweet to me you've been,
fulfill the longing to serve the giver
of the Bounty showered on me.

Afza... Ever Prolific

Oh Afza, from within Your Infinite Ocean,
You bring forth the creation of endless worlds,
stars, and creatures that swim and crawl
and fly in the sky and in their minds.

Master of the three worlds,
there is no end to Your Proliferation.

*Before the beginning
neither Nothing nor Everything existed
until You manifested Your Whim to know Yourself
and Nothing and Everything
were born in Your Infinite Ocean.*

*Both were ignorant, but everything needed to know,
and Nothing could not know without becoming Everything.*

Oh Afza, You have given us the Name for that place
where knowing clashed with not knowing.

Om, Om, Om.

Nasha... Reaching Equally to All

I am so lost within the dream of time and space
that it is impossible to see
how in the vastness of creation
Your Existence reaches equally to all.

Oh Nasha, could it be,
that the mystery of how
is revealed in Your words,
My dear,
You and I are not we—
but One.

Parwara... Nourisher

Because of You,
there is air to breathe,
water to drink,
and fire for transformation.

Because of You,
a generous planet—
the wayfarer's
home away from Home,
serves our every need and wish.

Oh Beloved,
as Afridgar[5]
You create,
as Fanakar
You desolve,
and as Parvardigar
You Sustain.

Oh Parwara,
You are Nourisher of all.

Inaha... Protector of the World

Protector of the world,
since You are everything and nothing is beyond You,
then what exactly are You protecting us from?

I think it must be Yourself.

As Brahma, You create,
as Shiva, You destroy,
and because there is destruction,
there must also be protection.

Oh Inaha,
through your constant vigilance
You Protect the World from Yourself.

Ain-aenah... Never-changing

Illusion ever changing,
a kaleidoscope of shifting forms,
and through these forms dance consciousness's
eternal pilgrimage to Your door.

Ain-aenah... Never changing,
pristine and immaculate You endure,

non-dual and imperishable.
in the state beyond Beyond.

An-aenah... Formless

Behind the curtain of creation,
the subtle world
enlivens and sustains,
silent servant of creation's blueprint
that the mental sphere maintains.

Beyond all forms exists the formless
and in the formless,
movements cease.

Oh mind, go to An-aenah and be still,
for in the formless there is peace,
and in that peace resides
the happiness you seek.

Kharoshid-tum... Most Steadfast Among the Steadfast

I am weak and wavering
on my journey to your door,
while steadfast the Pirs and Walis[6],
whose minds tyrannize them no more.

Among the steadfast stands the Pole,
beckoning all to come to Him,
Most Steadfast among the Steadfast,
in unwavering resolve.

Mino-tum... Lord Invisible

The yogi sits with his disciples
discoursing on the nature of thought.

"Thought is material," he says,
"and matter is not sacred."

My mind wanders as he speaks.
I begin to contemplate not his words
but the man himself.

He is sincere and tries to lead a pure life.
He restrains himself from passionate pursuits,
eats no meat, drinks no wine,
and keeps his thoughts concerned with sacred themes.

"Bring your thoughts to silence," I hear him say.
"Where thought ends the sacred begins."

I remember what my Beloved said.
"Things that are real are given and received in silence."

Oh Mino-tum,
none can see you but with eyes divine.

Oh Lord Invisible,
help this yogi attain the silence he seeks.

Vasna... All Pervading

In the beginning,
when You began to dream,
You dreamt Yourself
and became so identified,
You forgot Your Real Self.

The dreamer became the dream,
illusion was established in Reality.

When You finally awoke,
You became the Father,
and from the Father became the Son,
and from the Son, the Holy Ghost.

The dreamer became the dream,
Reality was established in illusion.

Self of self,
The All Pervading One
You are everything and everything is you,
nearer to me than my own breath.

Harvastum… All in All

All contains all,
Everything and Nothing too.

In the mirror of Nothing,
All that is Everything
sees nothing,
which it takes itself to be.

While in the mirror of Everything,
All that is Nothing
sees everything,
which it knows itself to be.

So Everything becomes Nothing,
and Nothing becomes Everything.

The Dreamer becomes the dream
and the dream becomes the Dreamer.

Oh Harvastum,
You became me
to know yourself as Nothing,
and find Yourself as Everything.

Oh All in All,
help me look into the mirror of myself,
so I may be effaced
in the love of my Beloved

Hu-sepas… Worthy of our profound thanks

Oh Hu-sepas,
thank You for this life You've given me lead,
for I am blessed to feel part of and participant in
Your Great Work of perfecting consciousness.

Only through this feeling of connection with You
does my life hold any
meaning to me at all.

I dedicate my life to You with gratitude and love.
May it always be
a worthy celebration
of Your Divine Compassion.

Har-Hamid... All Embracing Goodness

Har- Hamid,
Your very Being,
all Your actions and inactions,
absolutely pure and unsullied,
are expressed in the universe as
Your All Embracing Goodness.

Your Goodness is Your Perfection,
revealed in Your unwavering vigil
over Your Whim to know Yourself.

Oh Har-Hamid,
there is no stain upon the cloak of Your Goodness,
You are Divinely Honorable,
and worthy of our most profound respect.

Har-naik-faraih... All embracing Holy Light

With the surge of God's Original Whim in the Infinite Ocean,
a great friction between asleep and awake
transformed the Dark Mist into the fiery flames of Tej.

Tej, the Original Holy Light, passed through the prism of imagination
called Wahm,
and shattered into the Seven Original Holy Colors.

Each Color then divided seven times seven
and this continued seven times more,
until an infinite number of colors were manifested in creation.

All these colors were vibrations—
movement at different speeds,
and all these vibrations became the universe.

When the ear perceives vibrations,
we call it sound,

when the eye perceives vibrations,
we name it color,
when mind perceives vibrations,
we describe the phenomena as thought or feeling,

but when heart perceives the All-embracing Holy Light,
it is experienced as the Seeing of God.

Oh Har-naik-faraih,

Lord of life,
Light of lights,
You are the Goal and You are the Way.

Baish-tarana… Remover of Afflicition

Oh Baish-tarana,
what affliction is this
that causes my thoughts, words, and deeds
to miss the mark?

Why is there a sense of strange failure
in everything I do?

A great poet once asked,
"Could it be,
you have forgotten the Friend?"

Oh Remover of Affliction,
it is all right, by me,
if You decide to remove some of the affliction of my own ignorance,
but regarding the suffering caused by my longing for union with You,
I pray,
let that remain,
as lately I have become more and more drawn
to be in its company.

Taronish... Beyond Affliction

I can only imagine what it would be like
to be beyond affliction.

I think I would be intelligent.

I think I would be strong.

I think I would be happy.

Oh Taronish,
Infinite Consciousness,
Infinite Existence,
Infinite Bliss,

You are Eternally Free and Pure,
the Savior of the afflicted,
please help me to free myself
from the tyranny of the convulsions of my mind.

Anah aoshaka… Immortal

If there is birth,
death must follow—
every beginning
must have its end.

If there is appearance,
there must be disappearance—
creation withdraws into the void.

Oh Anah aoshaka,
You are beyond
birth and death,
beginning and end,
appearance and disappearance,
creation and dissolution.

Oh immortality,
is it true?
Can I find You in the space between
the in and the out of my own breath?

Farasaka... Fulfiller of Holy Desires

The Whim to know Yourself was the First Holy Desire
that began the dream where You went missing
to find Yourself again as me.

Now, impelled by the First Holy Desire,
like a ghost You haunt the dream
and through my weary voice I hear You pray,

Oh Farasaka, Fulfiller of Holy Desires,
may Your Divine Gaze be upon me,
the company of Your Sahavas be with me,
and may You allow me to take Your Blessings,
again and again, until the very end,
when I am worthy of union with You.

Pajohdehad… Creator of Holy Attributes

Never troubling anyone on one's own account,
a lucid mind, free of fear,
absolute reliance on God.

Love for God and belief in the Reality of Manifestation,
poise amidst all calamities and hardships,
cheerful,
indifferent to caste, creed and religious ceremonies,
trust in the state of be as it may.

Oh Pajohdehad, Creator of Holy Attributes,
help me find real happiness in making others happy.

Khwafar... Compassionate Judge

At every breath I stand before the Judge,
my conscience speaking to my mind.
"I don't want to hear this," says my mind.
"You've got it wrong."
"It isn't that way!"
"He did this and that is why…"
"I am justified!"
"I am right!"

Khwafar never argues,
just tells it how it is.
Conscience cannot be swayed by the convulsions of the mind.

Oh Compassionate Judge,
it is my mind that hears You,
but my heart that understands,
and patiently informs me
of Your Compassionate reminders.

Avakhshiaea… Merciful Giver

The golden chain that binds the saint to goodness,
and the spiked chain that shackles the sinner to pleasure and pain,
are both Your Merciful Gifts.

Heaven and hell,
loss and gain,
are Your Merciful Gifts.

The cloth, dipped in dye, emerges a vivid hue,
only to be faded in the sun,
and dipped again,
its brilliance regained.

Dipping and fading, until its color is fast,
again and again, until the color is fast.

Praise to You, Avakshiaea,
Merciful Giver,
Breaker of Chains.

Abaraja... Bountiful Giver

I have walked where You have walked,
though not in Your shoes.
I have been made to feel more than a guest in Your home
as I sat and listened to the Chosen Ones
tell stories of Your Life among us.

I have wept in joy at Your Samadhi.

I have been with You in dreams and visions,
and met the glowing faces of those blessed souls
transformed by the touch of Your Love.

Oh Abaraja, Bountiful Giver,
the greatest gift that You bestow
is the gift You give of the company of Your Very Self.

I entered the room, but saw You not,
and was convinced that You were absent,
until the fragrance of Your perfume betrayed You,
and this beggar learned the simple truth:
In Your game of hide and seek,
The Beloved may be hidden,
But the Beloved is never gone.

A-satoha... Unconquerable

The haughty king looks out his window
with distain at the beggar in the street below.

The self-pitying beggar looks up at the palace window
with envy and desire in his heart.

Both king and beggar, condemned by the Great Laws,
exchange their parts again and again,
for lifetimes on end,
until one day the sight of the beggar arouses the King to thoughts:

Both king and beggar I have been,
and whether my garb be royal or ragged,
in Reality,
Pure, Celestial, Soul,
I am.

And on that day also,
the beggar sees the king and thinks,

Both beggar and king I have been,
and whether my garb be ragged or royal,
in Reality,
Pure, Celestial, Soul,
I am.

Oh A-sataha,
the game of king and beggar is the Illusion
that sustains the Reality of Divine Oneness.

In the game, You play the roles of conqueror and conquered,
while in Reality You remain—
Unconquerable.

Rakhoha... *Freest of the Free*

You were Free,
the Freest of the Free,
beyond all qualities,
all attributes and forms,
action and inaction,
birth and breath,
life and death,
Everything and Nothing too.

But, You were asleep,
and knew neither Yourself nor Your Freedom.

So You set forth on Your Journey,
through the Ocean of Your Dreams,
traveling from shore to shore,
experiencing everything,
becoming everything,
becoming bound.

The King had locked Himself in His dungeon
and lost the key.
The dreamer became the dream,
but the dreamer's destiny was to awaken.

When You Awoke,
You saw it all had been a dream,
a pouring from the empty into the void,

and You were,
as You were before,
Free,
the Freest of the Free,
beyond all qualities,
all attributes and forms,
action and inaction,
birth and breath,
life and death,
Everything and Nothing.

You were Awake,
and knew Yourself.
You had become Rakhoha,
Freest of the Free.

Varun... Deliverer from Evil

Mind standing in the shadows of gloom,
wrapped in the cloak of darkness,
seeing wrong as right,
incapable of perceiving Truth,
or relinquishing sorrow and fears,
pessimism and despair—
this is wickedness and sin.

Oh Varum, Deliverer from Evil,
carry us from the shores of the Lands of Shadows
into the effulgence of Reality's Love and Truth.

A-farefah... Never Deceiving

I have heard it said that You are deceiving.
You say something will happen,
it seems it never does.

You say You will break Your Silence,
But who has heard You speak?

You say one thing,
and do another,
break promises,
or so it seems.

Oh A-farefah,
Never Deceiving,
is it my own mind that deceives me?
By Your Grace,
I'll be released.

Be-fareftah... Never Deceived

My mind deceives me because my mind is deceived.
It drinks from the Ocean of Nothing,
it is the child of Illusion.

My conscience awakens me and is never deceived.
It drinks from the Ocean of Everything,
it is the child of Reality.

Oh Be-fareftah,
You are the Conscience of creation,
the spark of Truth within us all,

Eternally Awake,
Merciful,
Never Deceived.

A-dui... One Without Second

Multiplicity inhabits duality,
spinning comparisons,
distinctions,
above and below.

Multiplicity inhabits duality,
Conjuring pure and impure,
rich and poor,
beauty and repugnance,
sanity,
insanity,
evil and good.

Oh A-dui,
"You are without beginning
and without end,
non-dual,
beyond comparison,
and none can measure You..."[7]

You are Absolute,
Immeasurable,
And Eternal.

You are
The One Without Second.

Kam-rad... Lord of Desire

When the Desire to Know Himself arose within the sleeping God,
He did not wake directly,
but journeyed form dream to dream,
and the Original Desire to Know Himself
was lost in a litany of endless desires.

The Original Desire was hidden,
but not destroyed.
It exists eternally as the Essence of all desires,
but is never satisfied through them.

*That is why in everything we do
there is that sense of strange failure.*

Oh Kamrad,
awaken within me, satisfy Your Original Desire
to Know Yourself.

Farman-kam... Decreer of Sovereign Desire

Of the Original Desire to Know Yourself,
I have heard You characterize it as a Whim
whose nature is absolutely free.

Whim is causeless,
it is not an effect,
and remains for me, still,
the deepest mystery.

Oh Farman-kam,
I am wondering,
do you even know the secret
of the causeless cause of the Whim?

Does the Decreer know the Source of the Decree?
And is the Decree the Desire
or the Cause of the Desire?

Oh Decreer of Sovereign Desire,
perhaps that is why You say,

"Mind cannot fathom me.
Do not try to understand me.
Just love Me."[8]

Aekh Tan... Soul Supreme

When the Whim disturbed
the Original Infinite Ocean,
and numberless soul-drops were formed
in the Ocean's whirl and swirl,
bubbles of mind, energy, and form
surrounded the drops
creating the illusion of separateness and independence.

Oh Aekh Tan,
You bestow upon each drop
the gift of love and courage
to drink the Ocean
and realize itself to be,
Soul Supreme.
Perhaps that is why You always remind us,
"You and I are not we, but One."[9]

A-faremosh... Never-forgetting

And so, to awaken, You began to dream,
and because Your dream was so lucid,
You forgot that it was a dream.
Because it all seemed so real,
You forget Yourself,
and are now convinced that You are Me.

As me,
You live the life of the Holy Ghost,
believing in the illusion
of life and death,
pleasure and pain,
loss and gain.

Now, I am beginning to feel, perhaps it is time
to lose Your taste for oblivion,
to stop being a ghost,
to remember Yourself?

Oh Never Forgetting,
as the Holy One in me,
isn't it time for You to assert Your State of Never-forgetting,
and allow Yourself to awaken in me?

Hamarna... Just Accountant

From the moment of my birth the record has been kept—
every thought, every word, and every deed.

When I die, my book will be handed over to You,
to tally and total, and publish the result,
and sculpt the shape of my next life.

Oh Harmarna,
though You are the Just Accountant,
I still feel a little uneasy because I have not always made the best
choices.

Oh Just Accountant, hear my plea,
Forward my record to the Avatar of the Age[10],
for He is full of Love and Mercy,
and may, I pray, take pity on my situation.

Sanaea... Knowing All things

When You awoke,
You became the Knower of Yourself,
and because You are Everything,
You became the Knower of All things.

Knower of the past, the present, and the future,
All Knowing,
Infinitely Knowing,
You are Sanaea, Knowing All things.

A-tars... Fearless

Fear exists within the dream,
born of the union of ignorance and illusion.

Oh A-tars,
In your Awakened state,
ignorance and illusion have been dispelled for You
and You have become the Lord of Everything and Nothing.

Only in the dream is there birth and death.
Only in the dream can one kill or be killed.
Only in the dream is there loss and gain,
pleasure and pain.
Only in the dream does fear exist.

Oh A-tars,
Fearless One,
You have become Immortal,
how can fear ever exist in You?

A-bish... Devoid of Pain

I have heard that actions create impressions
and consciousness of impressions
compels the impressions be experienced.

Impressions formed from faulty actions
leads to pain,
while impressions formed from lucid actions
leads to pleasure.

The Avatar of the Age has said,
*"The saint is bound by a golden chain,
the sinner by a spiked one,
but the goal is to be free of all chains."*

Oh A-bish,
You have achieved the active inactive state,
where neither pleasure nor pain exists.

Devoid of Pain,
You have become
the Perpetual Enjoyer of Infinite Bliss.

A-frajdum… Most Exalted One

Through words and deeds,
ceremonies and prayers,
angels and men have exalted
You as the Highest of the High,
the Soul of souls,
the Lord of lords,
and Master and Savior of all.

Limited by the limits of our consciousness,
we have attempted to imagine and conceive You,
to enshrine the Unenshrinable in our minds and hearts.

Oh A-frajdum, Most Exalted One,
in Your Mercy You have allowed us our worship,
in Your Compassion You have allowed us our prayers.

Ham-chun... Ever the Same

Oh Ham-chum,
Ever the Same,

You are the changeless center of change,
the still point of the revolving sphere,
and the Eternal Pole
around which the dervish weaves and whirls.

You are Stillness,
You are Peace,

You are the Silent Destination
of the consciousness of Souls.

Mino-satihgar... Invisible Creator of the Universe

From silence emerged sound,
from stillness the whirling spheres.
Out of Peace was manifested longing,
from Eternity, the illusion of time.

The Hand of Bliss rocked
the cradle of pleasure and pain,
Power cast its shadow of weakness,
and Ignorance donned Knowledge's cloak.

Oh Mino-satihgar,
Because of the Whim to know Yourself
You have become,
The Invisible Creator of the Universe.

A- minogar... Creator of the Profoundly Spiritual

From Your Deep Sleep You began to dream,
and You dreamt more and more,
and You became absorbed more and more,
until You went to the limit,
and then You turned back.

The Whim became conscious,
Your dream, Divine,
and You began to awaken.

Passing through numberless experiences
of sights, and sounds, and powers,
You became the mind,
master of thought,
and master of feeling.

Then You awoke and You were Nothing.
Nothing underwent the transformation to Everything,
and You took Your rightful seat on the Divine Throne.

But when You looked out upon the Kingdom of Yourself,
You noticed that You were still not free,
that the dreams from which You awoke continued to be,
and all the creatures and beings You had created,
were still mired in their illusory stories.

Oh A-minogar, Creator of the Profoundly Spiritual,
You took mercy upon Yourself,
and rejoined the dream to awaken Your reflection,
in all Your shapes and forms.

You became the Savior,
bound in Divine Responsibility.

You became Parvardigar,
Preserver and Protector of All.

Mino-nahab... Hidden Within the Spirit

When Your dream became Divine,
darkness began to long for the light,
and mind, ever active, began to slow,
and slow, and slow,
until it stopped.

Transformed into Spirit,
Spirit looked within and saw Self,
and merged with Self,
and Self awoke.

Nothing became Everything,
Darkness dawned into Light,
and Mino-nahab throwing off His Cloak,
revealed the Hidden Within the Spirit.

Adar-bad-gar... Transmuter of Fire Into Air

Somewhere within Your
deepest dreamless sleep,
mysteriously,
the Whim arose.

Heat from the friction between
that which was Destined to Know,
clashed with that which was Destined Not to Know
and You were profoundly disturbed.

Time was yet to exist,
yet Eternity passed.
The friction intensified,
Destined to Know
Awoke,
and from this Awakening
Fire manifested—The Fire of Tej.

The Fire of Tej engulfed Not Knowing,
and the Dream of Creation,
cloaked in Fire,
emerged from the flames of Tej.

Fire cooled into energy,
energy into space.

Space breathed itself
and became air.

Air condensed into water,
and water dissolved into earth.

Adar-nam-gar… Transmuter of Fire into Dew

Have you seen the dance of Fire,
its kaleidoscope of changing shapes,
whirling and weaving,
in a robe of shifting colors,
seeking its Beloved,
longing for Union?

Have you tasted the tears of Fire's longing,
in the clouds and in the rain,
in the oceans and the seas,
in the dew that gently weeps upon the earth,
in the morning when she wakes?

Oh Transmuter of Fire into Dew,
what kind of Wine have You wept
that in a single taste
both satisfies and creates
the desire for more Intoxication?

Bad-adar-gar... Transmuter of Air into Fire

The moth,
intoxicated with longing,
spirals around the flame,
closer, closer, and closer still,
until consumed by her desire,
becomes the fire itself.

The lover, mad with longing,
spirals around the Beloved,
closer, closer, and closer still,
until consumed by his desire,
becomes the Beloved Himself.

Bad-adar-gar,
Transmuter of air into fire,
make my mind burn with such longing for my Beloved
that it becomes one with Your Fire,
annihilated in the dance of Love.

Bad-nam-gar... *Transmuter of Air into Dew*

Thought without Cause is Whim,
Whim working in Ignorance is Wham[11],
Wham in the state of Remembrance is Longing,
Longing in the state of Rigor is Illumination.

As light withdraws into darkness,
warmth recedes into the coolness of night,
Remembrance is lost in Forgetfulness.

Forgetfulness begets sorrow.
Sorrow's tears fall as dew
upon the earth.

Bad-gail-gar... Transmuter of Air into Earth

You worshiped the great stone idol,
made in the image of Yourself.

You charged the great stone idol
with all the qualities You possess.

You bestowed life on the great stone idol,
Your own hidden perfection made it Divine.

Gazing into the mirror you saw Yourself,
but took the image to be another.

Reaching out,
You embraced the image,
the mirror shattered,
and You were embracing Yourself.

The great stone idol had dissolved into air.

But the journey was not yet complete,
Air was destined to be transmuted into Dust.

Bad-gerd-tum... Supreme Transmuter of Air into Dust

Imagination is the nature of air,
and air just goes on imagining
until it is transmuted into dust.

In dust there is no life,
Creation cannot exist without imagination.

Oh Bad-gerd-tum,
Supreme Transmuter of Air into Dust:

Transmute my imagination in the crucible of fire,
that I may become dust at my Master's feet
where no desire lives,
but the longing for union with Him.

Adar-kibritatum... Supreme Transmuter of Fire into Divine Sparks

After the Whim,
but before the Beginning,
friction burst into flames
that encircled the portal through which You,
cloaked in Your imagination,
were destined to emerge.

When You burst through that portal, flames caught hold of Your cloak,
and were flung as sparks
into the world of Your dreams.

When You awoke,
You looked back
and saw them,
and You were in awe!

Children of Tej,
charged with life from nearness to You,
had entered Your world.
Oh Adar-kiritatum,
from the moment You first saw them,
You have never forgotten their plight.
You have become their Savior
and bare eternal responsibility for all the Divine Sparks
still lost in the darkness of Your Original World.

Bad-agr-jae... Spreading Air Everywhere

As Divine Sparks we are children of the Original Fire,
and drops of the Infinite Ocean,
linked and sustained through breath.

Air is the food of breath.

Oh Bad-agr-jae,
Spreading Air Everywhere,
sustain us on our journey to awakening.

After the great snow,
He went out into his yard,
scattering crumbs of bread for the little birds
foraging for food on their homeward journey.

Ah-tum... Creator of Life-giving Water

Though always the same,
it makes its appearance
in numberless shapes and colors.

It is the blood of our planet,
transmitter of vibrations,
the river of life flowing within us.

It is the pure ocean that washes away all stains,
the great transparency,
and the great mirror also.

It is the essence of the subtle sphere.

Oh Ah-tum,
Creator of Life-giving Water,
we honor You in the baptisms of John,
awaiting Christ's transformation
of water to wine.

Gail-adar-gar... Transmuter of Dust into Fire

There is no life in the real dust,
it nourishes nothing,
sustains nothing,
and has no interest in anything.

All hopes and aspirations end in dust,
and by being useless in every way,
wins the heart of the Beloved,
Who turns it into Fire.

"Like waves upon my head the circling curls,
So in the sacred dance weave ye and whirl.
Dance then, oh heart, a whirling circle be.
Burn in that flame.
Is not the candle He?"[12]

Gail-vad-gar... Transmuter of Dust into Air

Oh Dust,
did you think that your journey was over,
when you found the feet of your Beloved?

You had become helpless and hopeless,
worthless in every way,
but did you think He would allow you to remain
in your pathetic state?

Did you think that your Lord would breathe dust?

Your journey ends in union with Him,
When, as air, He breathes you in,
transmuting Nothing into Everything.

Gail-nam-gar... Transmuter of Dust into Water

When violence took hold of the hammer of destruction,
and struck the idol in the darkness of the night,
the idol crumbled into dust,
to reform itself again,
by the dawn of morning's light.

When Love took hold of the hammer of destruction,
and struck the idol in the light of day's dawning,
the idol shattered into tears,
and tears flowed like rivers,
into the sea of Divine Union.

At the Inn,
The tavern keeper filled two goblets of wine,
for the enjoyment of his wife and himself,
on a warm summer's evening
when stars filled the sky,
and the fragrance of tuber roses perfumed the air.

Gar-gar... Master Craftsman

Master Craftsman,
as Dream Weaver,
You have fashioned the three worlds[13],
and within Your own creation,
You journey to Your own Awakening.

Mind, energy,
all manner of shapes and forms,
time and space,
You have crafted after Your own fancy,
and as me,
You look around and are amazed—
and deceived.

So crafty is Your handiwork,
You have forgotten it is dream.

Oh Gar-gar,
as the Awakened One,
You appear in the dream,
again and again,
to awaken Yourself.

Oh Master Craftsman,
do You ever fear
You have become too crafty for Your own good?

Garo-gar... Rewarder of Sincere Desires

Oh Garo-gar,
I have observed that there are times
when I would give almost anything for something,
yet after obtaining it,
wonder why I ever had any desire for it at all.

I have concluded, that I have no lack of desires,
but I do have a problem with self-deception,
and that self-deception precludes real sincerity.

Still, there are times when I think of my Beloved,
And long to be with Him,
in the places He has lived and laughed,
and, I am sure, that that desire is no dissimulation.

Oh Garogar,
it would be insincere of me to pretend I have no interest
in the reward of my insincere desires,
for I am still very much attached to illusion.

But please, in all sincerity,
take seriously my one real desire,

to love my Beloved more and more,
and more and more,
and still yet more,
till I am worthy of union with Him.

Gar-a-gar... Creator of All Humanity and Its Actions

God as His own creation,
appears in the world,
passionate and destructive,
lucid and kind,
sinner and saint,
as man and woman,
rich and poor,
healthy and sick,
sane and insane.

Oh Gar-a-gar,
Creator of all humanity and its actions,
I believe You revealed a great secret,
when, as Avatar,
You requested your blind lover
to touch Your cheek.
"See the closeness of Baba's shave," You said.
"Baba, I never thought about God shaving," he exclaimed.
"I am more human then you are," You replied.

Gar- a-gar-gar... Creator of All Human and Animal Life

Matter and energy,
form, space, and time,
has become the reality of Illusion,
while awakening to Reality—
only some fantasy cherished by the weak and deluded.

Oh Gar-a-gar-gar,
Creator of All Human and Animal Life,
I wonder what You might think,
when after millions of lifetimes,
ages and ages,
endless cycles of time,
You finally awake?

*"It was a beautiful dream,
perfect in every way,
but perhaps,
just a little too short."*

A-gar-agar... Creator of All the Four Elements

Fire came first,
the result of the Original Friction,
created within Your Whim to know Yourself.
After Fire came Air,
then Water,
then Earth.

We see their reflection in our world,
but they are not what they appear to be,
for they exist in worlds beyond our own.

The world of mind is mental,
and maintains the pattern of their existence.

The world of energy is subtle,
and energizes the pattern of their existence.

Oh, how little I know!

*"Earth, water, fire, and air,
met together in a garden fair,
put in a basket bound with skin.
If you answer this riddle You'll never begin."*[14]

A-gar-agar-gar... Creator of All the Planets and All Other Worlds

Creator of countless stars and planets,
whirling spheres of darkness and light,
the vastness of Your creation overwhelms my mind,
and I feel lost and insignificant.

Oh A-gar-agar-gar,
how is it that in the effulgence of Your creation,
You remain so humble?
Could it be
You know some great and hidden secret?

A-guman... Never in Doubt

As the great battle was about to commence,
Arjuna, beloved of Krishna, grew weak and indecisive.
In response, Krishna sang The Song Celestial and changed Arjuna to
A-guman.

Oh A-guman,
You are Never in Doubt because in Your heart You know a great
secret.

Live the life of action informed by lucidity,
unattached to success or failure,
praise or blame.

Know that you are not the doer or the done,
and dedicate all actions and their fruits to Me.

Cultivate detachment in involvement,
transform passion into love,
and always remember the words and the tune,
and the sound of My voice when I sing to you,
My Song Celestial.

A-jaman... Ageless

Krishna told Arjuna,
your worry is misplaced,
for neither are you slain nor can you slay.
You are deathless and changeless,
you are Spirit,
Immortal and Eternal.

The Beloved said,
When the spirit is absorbed in mind,
It dreams the dream of birth and death,
But when the mind is merged in spirit,
It sees the Self without beginning or end.

A-Khuan... Eternally Awake

All creation dreams the dream of sleeping and awakening.
The secret is this:
In deepest sleep we return home,
to imbibe the reality our original state.

The irony is this,
We arrive asleep
and never experience it.

Oh A-Khuan,
You have arrived awake in deepest sleep
and experienced consciously
the Reality of Your Home.

Oh A-Khuan
You have achieved the Eternally Awake state,
in which all need of sleep is vanquished.

Amast... Ever Alert

As the lover,
you remain ever alert,
keeping watch over your heart,
so no strangers enter your Beloved's abode.

As the God intoxicated wayfarer,
you remain ever alert,
to the Tavern wench as she weaves her way,
carafe in hand,
between the tables of thirsty souls.

.Oh Amast,
watchful over all creation,
as Sustainer, ever alert,
keeping Vigil while the world sleeps
in the conscience of our hearts.

Fashutana... Ever Protecting

How can there be a destination without a path,
a path without a journey,
an awakening without sleep,
and sleep without dreams?

Oh Fashutana,
to protect the Path to Yourself,
You became Parvardigar,
The Preserver and Protector of all.

Padmani... Recorder of Man's Actions

Nothing is hidden from You,
there is nothing You do not see,
and all You see You record,
In *The Great Book of All Actions.*

For You, the past is never forgotten,
and the future holds no surprise.

You are the most feared,
because your record of each man's actions,
determine his path through heaven or hell.

You are the Divine Accountant and at the appropriate time,
You hand over the records to the Savior,
Who reviews the account of each soul's journey.

And with the Quill of His Compassion,
dipped in the blood of His own heart's tears,
He relieves the debts of our forgetfulness
dispensing credits of His Love.

Firozgar... Victorious

Your Song Celestial,
inspired Arjuna to act
without attachment
to the triumph of victory
or the agony of defeat.
By dedicating his life at Your feet,
and wishing only to please You,
he became Victorious.

Oh Firozgar,
Help me to remember You,
in every thought, and word, and deed,
so that sense of strange failure
is vanquished from my life forever,
and awakening from the dream of myself,
I too become,
Victorious.

Kudawand... Lord of the Universe

Lord of all things seen or thought,
and all things unseen seen or unthought-of also.

Lord of all sentient and subtle beings,
and all consciousness that worships You.

Lord of the Province of Dreams,
Speaker of the Word,
Singer of the Song,

You are Kudawand,
Lord of the Universe,
arrayed in Celestial Robes,
Presider over the Festival of Life.

Ahuramazd... Lord of Life and Wisdom

In the homes of Your Holy Name, The Original Fire of Tej is
worshiped and maintained,
and the teachings of Your Holy Prophet, Zoroaster, inspires good
thoughts, and words, and deeds.

Oh Ahuramazd,
Lord Supreme,
in the home of Your beloved children
our Beloved was born and nurtured,
and for that,
we are infinitely grateful and endeared.

Oh Ahuramazd,
You came into existence
to hear the Original Word
and cradle the Original Whim,
when it manifested the wish to know.

Oh Ahuramazd,
Lord of Life and Wisdom,
we celebrate Your being
with cool tears—
Dancing Sparks of the Fire of Tej.

Abarin-kuhan-tawan... Preserver of Creation

As the Awakened One,
You remain always aware
of those numberless souls
still trapped in Your Dream,
and You are not indifferent to our plight.

Now, some have suggested,
"Just end the Dream,"
but to this You say,

"By Preserving the Dream,
you are given the opportunity to awake."

Oh Abarin-kuhan-tawan,
at what cost do You Preserve the Dream,
so that we may dream the dream of awakening?

Oh Preserver of Creation,
at what sacrifice do You return again and again,
awake into Your Dream
to Preserve our awakening by preserving Creation?

Abarin-nao-tawan... Renewer of Creation

All creatures in creation return to sleep
to touch the Source and Goal of Existence
and renew the dream of life.

Abarin-nao-tawan,
Renewer of Creation,
through Your Gentle Song,
mighty Brahma was enticed to sleep,
and in His sleep
Creation slept
and dreaming ceased.

Abarin –nao-tawan,
Renewer of Creation,
through Your Gentle Song,
Mighty Brahma stirred from sleep,
begins again to dream,
and a renewed and eager
creation yawns,
and wakes
once more to life's adventure.

Vaspan... Embracing All Creation

It is my prayer
that when from time to time
You hear the call of Five in One[15],
and take a human form
to live among us,

let it be my fortune
to be with You,
to see Your face,
to hear Your voice,
and feel Your embrace.

That Eternal embrace,
a brief respite,

safe harbor of love,
from the ocean's strife,
that plagues my journey home.

Vaspar… Giver of All Things

Giver of pleasure, giver of pain,
giver of loss, giver of gain,

giver of fortune, giver of fame,
giver of freedom, giver of chains.

Giver of the sacred and the profane,
giver of drought, giver of rain,

giver of night, giver of day,
giver of work, giver of play,

giver of blame, giver of praise…

Khawar... Infinitely Patient

Age after age,
You stand in our midst
and give Your divine call,

"Come all unto Me."

Age after age,
You see us approach,
only to divert our glance,
and demure Your intimacy.

In my dream You tossed the ball to me and I caught it.
You tossed it again harder, and I returned it to You.

Again and again You tossed the ball,
harder and harder still.

It ricocheted off of ceiling, walls and floor.
I leapt and dove, caught it every time,
returning it to You with joy and pride.

When You stopped throwing,
we were standing very close,
and in Your silent smile,
I experienced an intimacy
I had never known—
and I was afraid.

"I guess we should return to the others who await You?" I said.

You looked so disappointed,
I knew my words had wounded You deeply.

You disappeared and I awoke,
my face wet with tears of sadness and regret.

Ahu... Lord of Existence

Oh Ahu,
You manifest Your Existence
in the starry world,
in angelic realms,
and in the whirling dance
of the lover and Beloved.

Five spheres of existence
manifest your Being,
that in the end,
You may come to know Yourself
as Love.

Oh Ahu,
Lord of Existence,
You are the Reality of Everything,
Existent within Existence.

Avakhshidar... Forgiver of Sins

Sometimes I think I see clearly,
sometimes I am quite sure,
I see nothing at all.

*How is it that in my thoughts and words and deeds,
I always seem to miss the mark?*

Oh Avakhshidar, Forgiver Of sins
A doctor can numb the pain,
but only You can remove the stain.

*Help me live my life in a way that pleases You,
according to Your Wish as well as Your Will.*

*I pray, You are and always will be
my Master, till the very end,
when I am worthy of union with You.*

*I pray for Your Love,
obedience to You,
and for a pure and lucid mind and heart.*

*I beg Your Forgiveness for any thought or word or deed
that has displeased You or caused you trouble,
and I pray, You help me to receive Your Forgiveness.*

I beg Your Forgiveness for my forgetfulness,

my distraction, and my sleep,
and I pray, You help me to awaken,
and attain the state of Remembrance of You.

I pray that Your Divine Nazar[16] *be upon me,*
till the very end, when I am worthy of Union with You,

that the company of Your Sahavas be with me,
till the very end, when I am worthy of Union with You,

and I pray, You allow me to take Your Darshan,
now and again and again,
until the very end,
when I am worthy of Union with You.

Dadar... Divine Creator

Divine Creator,
of the three worlds
and of all beings You are.

Not the mind, but that which makes the mind work,

not the powers, but that which empowers,

not the enchantments, but that which enchants,

not the gods, but that which makes them godly,

not the angels, but that which gives them wings,

not all beings, but that which gives them life,

not the dream, but the dreamer,

not the breath, but the breather,

You are.

Oh Dadar, Divine Creator,
all trains arrive and depart Your Station.

Please see that when we leave upon our journey,
a return ticket is safely in our hands.

Raiyomand... Rayed in Glory

From Your Infinite Eternal Being,
resplendent and magnificent,
stream beams of radiant light,
that cloaks You with the starry firmament,
and celestial songs that sing Your Glory.

You are the Source that feeds the stream
of worship and devotion,
of men and gods,
angels and beings divine.

Life and death bow to Your Feet,
Time prays to Your Eternity,
the eyes of all existence,
gaze upon You with the light Your effulgence.

"At the banquet of my heart[17],
From Your Face a light does shine,
Light as of a hundred lamps,
Pure, Resplendent, and Divine."

Khorehmand... Haloed in Light

Light Haloes Itself in Light,
reflected from the Mirror of Self,
and from that Orb of Light are flung lights celestial,
and from the lights celestial are lit the lamps terrestrial,
that are but shadows cast behind those soul beams,
as they journey along the path to Glory.

Oh Khorehmand,
may it be my destiny to become one of those soul beams
who form the circle of light that haloes You in Effulgence.

Two perfect mirrors look into each other,

What do they see?

"The glass is thin, the wine clear,
Where can a distinction be made?
For it appears that there is wine and yet no wine glass there,
Or that there is a wine glass and no wine there."[18]

Davar... Lord of Justice

Knowing everything,
You stand impartial,
seeing every effect's cause,
You remain unmoved.

Neither righteous nor unrighteous are judged on reputations,
and all who stand before You,
both the arrogant and the supplicant,
are treated with measured fairness.

Blind to beauty and ugliness,
unimpressed by powerless power,
deaf to excuse or explanation,

You are Davar, Lord of Justice,
Decrier of reward and punishment,
Cloaked in reason,
Crowned with compassion's stars.

Kerfaigar... Lord of Just Rewards

"The saint is bound with a golden chain.
The sinner is bound with a spiked chain.
The goal is to be free of all chains."[19]

Oh Kerfaigar, Lord of Just Rewards,
grant us the reward of freedom from all rewards,
So that we attain the Eternal Reward,

Sat, Chit, Ananda,
Union with You.

Bokhtar... Liberator

Free us from ignorance and the tyranny of fear,
emancipate us from the powers of lust, anger, greed,
hatred, jealousy, selfishness, and pride.

Oh Bokhtar,
Awaken us from the world of dreams,
destroy our illusions,
and liberate our spirit from the bondage of our minds.

Farsho-gar... Awakener of Eternal Spring

Weary from lifetimes of journeying,
beaten down by wind and rain,
scorched by desert's sun,
hungry,
thirsty,
unable to rest—
the wayfarer journeys on,
uplifted and sustained,
comforted and renewed by Your Gift
of Hope, and Love, and Faith.

Oh Farsho-gar, Awakener of Eternal Spring,
with Your right hand You hold the cloth in the burning sun,
until its color is all but bleached away.
Then, taking the cloth in Your left hand,
You dip it in the Dye of Self,
and it emerges in radiant colors Divine.

Dipping and fading,
again and again,
till the color is fast,
the journey complete,
and the wayfarer Awakens
in the Garden of Eternal Spring.

Endnotes

[1] *Khordeh Avesta*, trans. Maneck Fordoonji Kanga (Bombay: Trustees of the Parsi Panchayat Funds and Properties, 1993), pp. 405-409; *Khordeh Avesta: Zoroastrian Prayer Book with Prayers in Roman Script and Translation in English*, trans. T. R. Sethna (2nd edition, Karachi: Ma'aref Printers, 1975), pp. 208-210.

[2] A current translation in modern Persian is available in *Khordeh Avesta*, trans. Husayn Vahidi (Tehran: Bunyad-i Farhangi-i Surn Surushiyan, 1989), pp. 7-8.

[3] For the 99 divine names in Sufi practice, see my *Guide to Sufism* (Boston: Shambhala Publications, 1997), chapter 4.

[4] The Old Persian term for Worthy of Worship is *yazad*, or in modern Persian *izad,* are both derived from the Avestan term *yazata*, "adorable," found as a description of God in the *Gathas* of Zoroaster. Meher Baba retained this name (with the spelling Ezad) in the conclusion of his Universal Prayer.

[5] Afridgar, Parvardigar, and Fanakar – the Sufi terms equivalent to the Brahma, Vishnu, and Shiva (Vedantic) i.e. Creator, Preserver, and Destroyer.

[6] Spiritually advanced souls on the higher planes of consciousness.

[7] From the Parvardigar Prayer of Meher Baba

[8] From quotes by Meher Baba

[9] A quote by Meher Baba

[10] Avatar = the Christ, Messiah, Rasool.

[11] Divine Imagination

[12] Attributed to the 13th. Century poet Jalal al – Din Rumi

[13] The Gross, Subtle, and Mental Worlds.

[14] A line from a song by the Incredible String Band

[15] A reference to the five perfect masters that precipitate the advent of the Avatar.

[16] Gaze

[17] From the Persian poet Hafiz

[18] From the Arab poet Abu Nuswas found in *Mishkat Al- Anwar* by Al-Gazzali

[19] From a quote by Meher Baba